THE
POWER OF
POSITIVE THOUGHT

Summary

Hello everyone Michael Lee Kilmartin, I am an Author and creator of my Michael Say's series. I want to thank all of you for making my stories, and novels a success worldwide.

I now bring to you another inspiring new novel called The Power of Positive Thoughts. I will take you through my steps in how I developed a successful career with my company The Kilmartin Organization Inc.

My story will inspire you as everyone needs a push from time to time including myself to become the successful person that you would like to be, it just takes that first step to lead you to the right step.

You do not need to be rich to be happy and successful. Follow me and you will learn how to better yourself with a positive thoughts.

Dedication

I Michael Lee Kilmartin hereby, dedicate my books, and my series of short stories to my daughters Kristi and Lori. They inspired me to write my stories way back when they were just children.

The oldest is Kristi with my two granddaughters "Thank You, Kristi"

I can remember when I would read my stories to them and how they were so excited and how they laughed at the stories that I read to them. Which gave me such joy, I sure miss those days Kristi and Lori I Love You Both Always, Your Father.

From The Author

Hello Everyone, I wish to introduce myself, my name is Michael Lee Kilmartin. I am a United States Citizen and a California native.

My heritage and background are Scot, and yet some part of me is Irish. I grew up in a little country town, called Moorpark, California.

I have traveled the world as an Entrepreneur, Businessman, Optimist, and Philanthropist for the last forty years with my company The Kilmartin Organization Inc.

I have seen the world for its beauty and its people and its interesting and beautiful places, which gives me many creative ideas to write and publish my novels, children's stories, and science fiction stories. My motto Reach for the Stars, Never, Ever Give Up.

CONTENTS

CHAPTER

1

Did you ever look at yourself in the mirror, and say what am I doing here in this job? And then you say to yourself, I would like to make a change but I do not know where to start.

I am making a decent living, and yet I am not happy with what I am doing, I am always irritable when I get home to be with my family.

I have spent many years of my life learning to be in business with the company I am with; trying to get ahead in my career, and yet I have found that if I am promoted in my career I may add more stress to myself in a business I do not like.

Well everyone I am in the business of offering services in helping people in their businesses. I have taken many steps in my business to find the right steps to success.

I will now guide you through those steps. I found that it is an education in taking many steps and yet each step is a learning experience and I have gained knowledge and experience that has been very valuable in my career.

I have stumbled many times but I never gave up. I did realize in time that those steps were just stepping stones to my success.

I have found a very satisfying career and that is working for myself. I have developed many businesses over my lifetime that are now my DBA's to my company The Kilmartin Organization Inc.

Many of us get off on the wrong track where we wanted to go and end up in another direction altogether, either because we thought that it was the right way or the easy way.

When in fact it was the right direction at the time because it is a learning process that may take years to find success when you are growing up.

But with my help and guidance, you will learn the steps to take to be a success. But before I continue, here is one of the successful companies that I own and developed from the ground up called Natures Earth.

This venture became a national and international skin care line business a SUCCESS.

I did not know how to develop it at the time or have any help from the outside. Except with my education and existing customers and clients that gave me their support in being successful.

They would say if anyone could do it that would be Michael Lee Kilmartin. I am not patting myself on my success of building my business, well maybe a little and you can do it too. You just need to have the confidence and positive thought and attitude to make it happen.

CHAPTER

2

Now back to my story, are you getting the picture of what can happen if you make the right steps? It is going to take some guts to make it happen and it will not happen overnight, but you must have confidence that you can do it.

You will see dreams that come true, and that will change your life. Because dreams do come true, do not let anyone fool you that they cannot, because mine did. I dream a lot to make things happen in my life.

Ok on with the show, in my steps to success. Now maybe you are the employee that loves his job; are you one of those that would love to be promoted to become a leader in the business that you are working for?

OK so you are but you seem to be passed over for promotion all the time, but have you learned why that is happening?

Now this is important, are you working for a company that is a large corporation with lots of potential for promotion?

Or a small company with 50 or fewer employees. If it is a large corporation then why are you not getting promoted? is it a lack of education and a degree, experience, or all of the above?

Or maybe you do not have enough drive and ambition to get ahead, and you are not asking for that promotion, and maybe the company sees it.

Well in my business I have always preferred experience and am a beginner with a lot of ambition to do the job.

They are trainable and they can learn the business with training as they stay with the company, it is all up to you.

Remember education and training are everything and the companies that pass over experienced people, are making a big mistake because they have no degree. Talent and experience make money for you, not a degree.

Maybe you do not have the drive, you need to change that now and become a tiger and take on any project that is given to you with excitement and ready to make it happen "learn the job inside and out"

You will advance in taking on more responsibility and you will have a better chance of learning the business by doing so. Verses being stuck in the department where your learning abilities have stopped.

Remember now companies need aggressive people to get the job done, no matter how much work you may be doing more than others, if this is the case then did you ever wonder why?

They may be testing you to see if you can handle the challenge of a higher and new position. It is like running a race, do you want to be the winner or the loser? Then think positively that you can win and downshift into second gear and go for the winner's circle.

Step one sit down and create an outline of your strengths and weakness. This is vital if you want to understand where you should begin your quest for success.

Once you have written down all of your strengths and weak points you will have a bigger picture of who you are and what you need to concentrate on to make the next step.

Now simplify that list down to say 10 and the really important things on the list that make you happy. Start to look them over and over and memorize what they are. Do you see something on your list that you may like that you would want to explore? If so explore them and read up on what you need to do.

Next, do you have the qualifications to go further with the points of interest that you have found?

Such as the education and experience in a job that would match those points of interest. because you if do not have the qualifications then you may need to go back to school if you wish to stay with the company.

CHAPTER

3

Hi Sparky, my dog is in my series called Shorty and Sparky's Adventures. Yes, I am an Author too. Google my name and you will see the many books that I have written.

Writing is another career and a step that you can do as well as a part-time job, and when you become good at it a full-time job. I find it very soothing and exciting to write about something that I like, and in my case, it has been animals, when I first started.

Technology today is amazing in what you can do to find just what you're looking for right on the computer.

It is the key to having questions answered, in what you may be thinking about. Apply yourself and go on the computer and start asking Google the many questions that you wish to be answered.

You will be very surprised by what you will find on Google. Did you find a career that matches those questions? Boy,

I sure wish I had the technology and opportunities way back when I first started my business. My picture of how to do it would have been much clearer, and brighter for me.

In my own business and career, the opportunities are endless, if you know where to look for them. Next, you need to be honest with yourself in taking the next step, and that is you need to ask yourself, where will this next step take you.

Because to see the next step, you need to understand the next step completely in what you are going to be doing from this point on.

Then you need to continue to break down the questions and points of interest on your list into smaller pieces until you have a complete understanding of those questions.

Step two, did you ever think of starting a business of your own? I can remember when I started my first company Sales Unlimited and that was because I was laid off from the company back then.

When a layoff took place in the company, a very scary time for me. Yet I was a top salesman and their top district manager for the company in San Diego, California at that time.

This was such a letdown for me because; I was on the street the same day the announcement was made to me, with no warning that it was going to happen or time to look for another job.

But did you know that was "the best thing that ever happened to me" even though I was scared to death about what I was going to do for work and income and support?

Well, I went home and started to figure out a plan for what I would do from this point on in my life.

Well, an idea came to me in and that was why not start my own business, not saying for you to quit your job and start a company as I did. After several months of interviewing with companies, and starting all over with several offers that were given to me.

You need to research what type of work you would qualify for, do not make a rash decision and quit your job and start a company unless you have qualified yourself to be able to take such a giant step.

This is very important that you are thinking of a career in something that you can understand and manage and one that you will enjoy.

Now when I was laid off I did have many years in retailing and sales, which gave me a foothold, in what I was going to do for a career.

Now stand back and say what kind of background, experience, and education you have. You do not need a degree to be successful, only if you are working with a company that requires one.

Now have you done the research on Google that will answer the questions on your list? And a career that you are sure you would like to do?

I know it is another step, granted but hopefully, many questions will be answered in your research. Getting back to step one, let's say that you wish to continue to work in your present job and you are not ready to start your own business.

CHAPTER

4

How about this do you have the time to start a sideline part-time business? Meaning you will still keep your present job, and you will start a part-time business from your home.

I know you are working too many hours already, but if you want to be successful it takes many hours and steps to find the right path to success, it is not an 8-5 job.

But in the long run, it will pay off, just like graduating from college, it was fantastic was it not a gratifying feeling to graduate? This same feeling in discovering your right path to success as well can be achieved.

By the way, I started my first business called Sales Unlimited from my apartment when I lived in San Diego, California after several months of looking for a job. And when I did get an offer of one, it was no better than the I one I had. I would have to start all over again to prove myself.

So with my new company, I started calling on the same customers. Now is that not a cool thing for me, well I thought it was.

Because I gained back my self-respect back and self-confidence in what I had lost and I called on my customers for several years with my new business. Do you have a similar situation to this?

If so then start to pursue something in the same line of work or different that you can sell to them and remember it cannot be the same products.

It will be a conflict of interest, you can get into some serious trouble doing this until you quit and decide to go out on your own with your new business.

By the way in my first company, I became a manufacturer representative representing many companies, to begin with on straight commission. A tuff way to start, but it finally did start to pay off for me.

Owning your own company is a fantastic feeling. You become your boss, and you build something for yourself. Although be prepared to work long hours. It is not an 8-5 job.

I know you need money to start your own business which is understandable. Far as having money to start the business or seed money to keep you to get going until you are making enough to support yourself and your family.

Do you know how to make and set up a business plan? Very important when starting your own business, it is a plan, of how to begin a business from the beginning.

Your valuable knowledge and experience are worth money that you can take to the bank to get a loan. I was smart enough to own several rentals in San Diego at the time; I sold one of the rentals that I owned on the advice of my realtor and property manager and used the money to start my business. Now if you do not have the assets to do this, how about this do you own your own home?

If so then take out a second for whatever amount you feel that you need, or refinance the home as long as there is enough equity there to do so. Now if you were

like me and have rentals. I would say take out a loan against one, continue to collect rental income, and not sell it, continue to collect rent. I did not know enough about real estate back then to do that, otherwise, I would have refinanced the rentals and taken out a loan on one of them. Well, I changed that very quickly, I became a realtor and a mortgage broker. I wanted to know everything about my business to create and build my business.

CHAPTER

5

I am a multi-tasked businessman and I am proud of being one, it creates a solid base for my clients and customers, and a wonderful feeling that I can give them what they want, I like being a one-stop shop.

Now if you are not sure that you want to do this, then take your business plan to the bank and get an SBA loan, banks are lending money now because our president wants to see more businesses here in the USA that is startups, to build the economy.

Meaning people in business that wish to start their own business and an excellent way to get started without worrying about an income coming in when you quit your job.

The SBA loan is a government assistance loan to all new businesses that wish to start a business, it will be a lot of paperwork to get one, but it will be worth it once you get it.

I have had several SBA loans over my lifetime and career.

By the way, I am in my seventies and I believe age is only a number, as long as you stay in shape and do not think about retiring "I will not" Continue to make it happen and go for it and see the sparks fly when you get started.

The thrill of it all, that's what it is all about. Be positive, and do not think negatively. Life is too short to give up, and retire. People think that when they retire they would see the world and enjoy life, not true.

To me, that is a quick way to death. I have two brothers that retired in their fifties and they are younger than I, and they are not doing well, and one has just passed away just two years ago and the other is on his way.

I have tried for years to motivate them with my success. I will miss my brother, but I hold my head up high and I will continue my quest to help others.

Everyone owning your business is what is called an adventure, why give up and not think about making a new venture come true?

All with a positive attitude and thought that you can do anything if you put your mind to it, even at the age

I am now. It is very exciting to see things unfold and become a reality, and I love it. Every day is my goal to make something happen in my life.

It is a great feeling when a new idea comes to my mind, for my business. I begin to get more excited the more I think about it, and I begin my steps toward the next goal that I have been dreaming about.

I am a people person and you can be one as well. Having lots of friends will help you in your career.

The word gets out that you are looking to do something different with your life, and you will be surprised how many of your friends will give you pointers and ideas. Listen to them with open eyes and ears, and be a follower. I have learned many things from just listening to many of my friends and peers that I worked with and have met some that are very successful.

Just like when I was laid off, I discussed this matter with many of my clients and customers. They gave me ideas to start my own business back in the sixties, yes a long time ago.

Well, it paid off even though I made many steps to get where I am today. But do you know those steps were excellent in the right direction to a successful career?

Many of those steps became many DBAs of my business such as a real estate and finance company that I started called Financial Bankers Inc.

It has been a blessing to me to be able to buy and sell my own homes and properties, and to finance them with my knowledge of the business.

CHAPTER

6

You can do it too. You may sell a home or do a mortgage along the way for others or yourself if you have no desire to be in real estate, not everyone can be a salesman.

The opportunities are endless even today, in fact even easier today with the technology and trade schools out there. Just go for it and make it happen, and do not worry if you can do it or not.

Education is another secret to success, and without it, you will go nowhere. Education in learning a craft is very important and you must have a positive attitude to do it.

Negativity is everywhere, so stay away from those that are that way, stick with the winners and you will grow.

I love animals and I have written many books about animals that are the characters in my stories, like Shorty and Sparky Adventures Series.

They are my friends and family. I have five dogs and two cats in my family since my daughters are grown and making their own lives now.

They give me comfort when I am writing a new story about them. It is a great feeling to love animals and to write stories for children. Everyone should have an animal of some type; they can ad such enjoyment to your life.

Are you beginning to feel a positive feeling and are you starting to get the picture of what I am writing? I certainly hope so, as time will make it happen if you have the motivation to make it happen.

What is motivation in how you see it is something, like more money most of us would like to have. But did you know money comes with a drive to make it happen, yes it does the more you work at it the more you learn to be a go-getter, with a drive to make it happen?

CHAPTER

8

Does money drive you to be successful, well I do not feel that way money comes with knowledge from learning your craft? The better you get the more others will want more of what you have to offer.

Like when I started writing my books, I did not know if anyone would like books, but I did it anyway. Because it is something that I love to do and it gave me a positive feeling. I like to express myself when I am talking to my friends and family.

I have spoken and made many presentations in front of groups with my cosmetic business, boy was it that scary feeling to do so for the first time.

Well, I got up in front of people, many times and there would say around two hundred to explain my story of how I developed my Nature's Earth Skin Care Line.

It was not easy to stand up there and look back at all the people I was making my presentation to.

Like when I made a presentation to a large grocery chain called Safeway Stores, well I made my presentation to them with a few stumbles here and there.

But I managed to get through it, and I did say to them that was my first presentation to so many people.

You know when I finished my speech they stood up and applauded me for making the presentation, and I landed the account for my company.

After that, it was easy to do over and over with many other accounts from then on. "Just go for it"

Practice makes perfect is certainly a term and a quote that is so true. Where there is a will, there is a way. I have learned each step of the way in building my business to make a difference.

You must have a positive attitude to be successful, to see yourself as successful, and to be proud of yourself.

Life can be cruel at times when you are climbing the ladder. Because the world is a dog-eat-dog world out there.

But if you avoid the negativity such as watching the boob tube, as I call it, and each time when I turn it on.

The news is usually all about negative thoughts such as the president doing this and doing that with so many negative thoughts on every channel about him and what he has to say about our country.

My advice turn it off and not watch it because the world is yours if you work to make it that way. Forget about what others are doing and saying, just do your thing.

Now there are people that you can listen to and those people that are successful, like Jeff Bezos now that is another true Entrepreneur that also started his business out of his garage.

I can remember when he stood up on a talk show in the past and he would say, "I will have one of the largest companies in the world with my company Amazon.

Well, he was correct in what he had to say and he continues to make things happen because he loves it. What a positive vision he has, just pick up one of his books and see how he did it, and you will pick up some additional pointers on how to do it as well.

There are many Entrepreneurs out that you can follow. Which may be the path you may wish to take, so look them up and follow them. Think about it who you would like to be like.

Go on Google and look for him or her and see what they do to make it happen, and you will be surprised by what you may discover that will insure you even more ways to reach your goals. You will learn a great deal from just being a follower.

I assure you that there is nothing more enjoyable than to make someone feel good about themselves, does everyone have that opportunity to make it happen or feel it when it does happen?

Sad to say it only comes when you help others to see it. I get a kick out of being with children I will go places just to see them and be with them.

Like the parks, where you see them playing with other children, it is such a wonderful feeling just to be around them.

CHAPTER

10

Another place I enjoy going to is the bookstores, and the children's sections like Barnes & Noble, a very beautiful worldwide store. I see the children playing there with their toys and reading their storybooks to their mothers and fathers.

By the way, you can see many of my books on their websites and in their stores, where they advertise them.

I sure can remember those days. When my daughters were just children, I would come home, and one of the first things they want me to do is play with them; be it coloring in a coloring book, or going out to the park to swing them before dark, and another is to read to them a favorite story before bedtime.

You too can learn from others from just an idea that you may have, they will offer suggestions on a way to start a new venture with that idea of yours.

Now this is with positive thinking people only, you can help those that are negative later. When you are successful and on your way up.

Surround yourself with winners and successful people and be a sponge, and listen to what they have to say. You will be surprised by what you can learn from them by just being with them and listening to what they have to say; now everything may not be a positive feeling, but just stay with the positive words that they are saying.

Have you decided where you would like to go? find an entrepreneur that is in the same line of work, and follow them in how they built their business, like me in my following Donald Trump. Now no negative thoughts about me following him. I can remember way back when he wrote his first book and I picked up one and started to read about him.

His story of success is very inspirational and I began to read many of his books, even when I was building my business and flying all over the world. I became a follower of his writing while I was traveling.

Well, everyone that is the end of my story until my next volume and chapter in my life and I hope everyone learned something from what I have had to say and begins to follow my steps.

I know it is a lot to remember. Keep the book close by and go over it again and again until it sinks in since it is a fast-paced story that you can see is not a long story to absorb. I look forward to seeing you again in my next issue and novel.

Goodbye everyone, stay positive and happy, and go for the next step Michael Lee Kilmartin.

The End

No The Beginning

www.ingramcontent.com/pod-product-compliance
Lightning Source LLC
Chambersburg PA
CBHW071237220526
45468CB00002B/891